NATIONAL GEOGRAPHIC

D0503809

Fall Colors

Santina Bruni

Leaves change color

un the fall.

red leaves

orange leaves

yellow leaves

brown leaves

What colors are fall leaves?

red

orange

yellow

brown